FRANKLYN M. BRANLEY

and night

pictures by
HELEN BORTEN

THOMAS Y. CROWELL COMPANY
NEW YORK

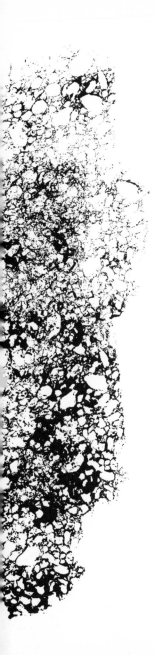

You live on the planet earth.
I live on the earth.
We all live on the earth.

The earth is round.

The earth looks like a big, big ball.

A ball is a sphere.

A sphere is something round all around.

The earth is a sphere. The earth is round all around.

3

If you were far, far, out in space the earth would look
like this.

You can see how big it is.

The red dot is New York City.

Many boys and girls live in New York City.

The black dot is San Francisco.

San Francisco has a big bridge.

The white dot is Denver.

Cowboys live on ranches near Denver.

The water is blue.

Trees and grass are green.

The land is brown.

The clouds are white.

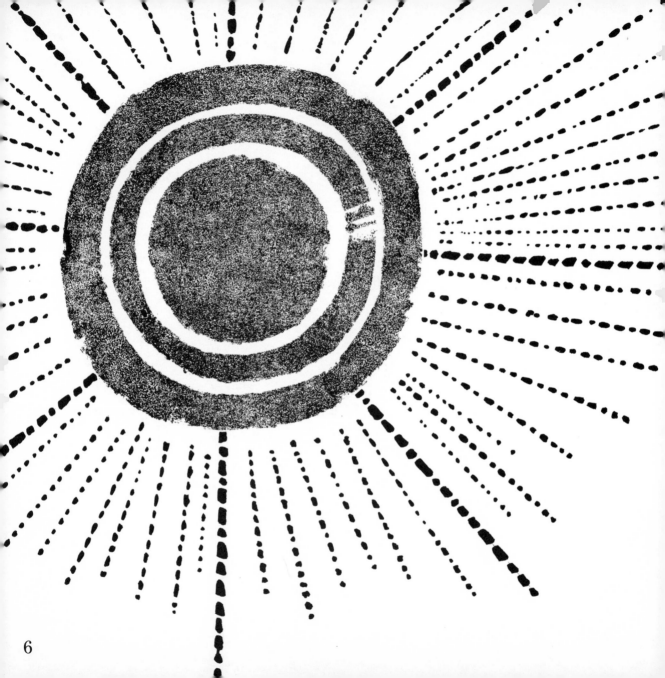

6

If you were miles and miles out in space the earth
    and the sun would look like this.
Sunlight falls on one half of the earth at a time.
That half is light. It has day.
The other half is dark. It has night.
When one half of earth has sunlight, the other
    half of earth is dark.

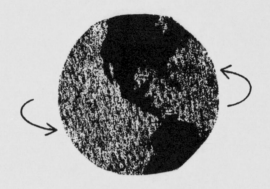

The earth turns around once a day.
You turn with the earth, but you cannot feel that
   you are moving.
As the earth turns, some people see sunrise.
That may be when you get up.

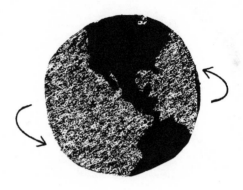

As the earth turns, some people see sunset.
That may be your bedtime.

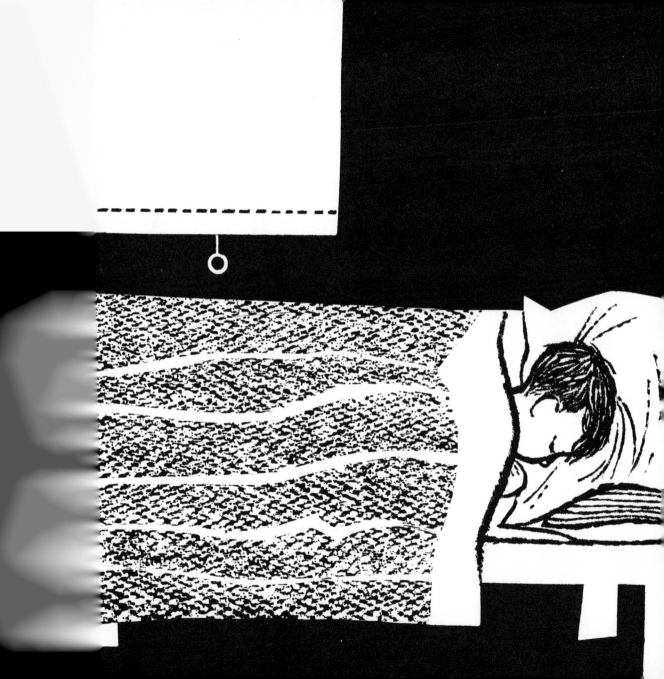

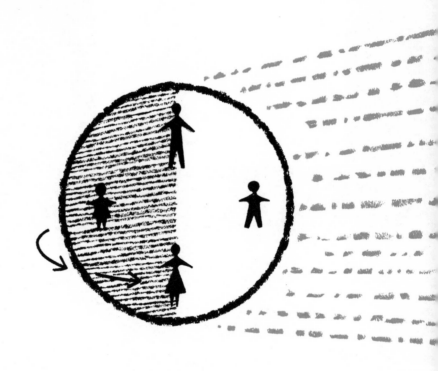

The arrows show the way the earth turns.
The sun shines on the boy. It is day for him.
No sun shines on the girl. It is night for her.

The man sees sunset. Earth takes him away from sunlight.
The woman sees sunrise.
Earth takes her toward sunlight.

The earth is a sphere.

The earth is always turning. It never stops.

It takes the boy away from the sunlight. The sun does not shine on him. Now it is night for him.

It takes the girl into sunlight. The sun shines on her. Now it is day for her.

As the earth turns, it takes the man toward the sunlight. Now it is sunrise for him.

As the earth turns, it takes the woman away from the sunlight. Now it is sunset for her.

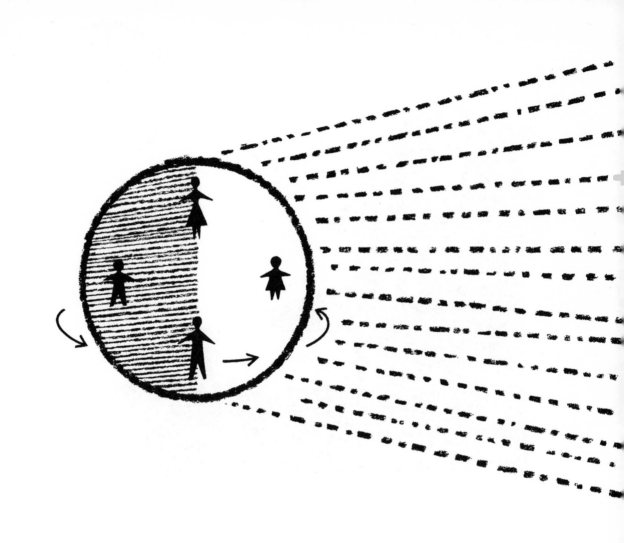

15

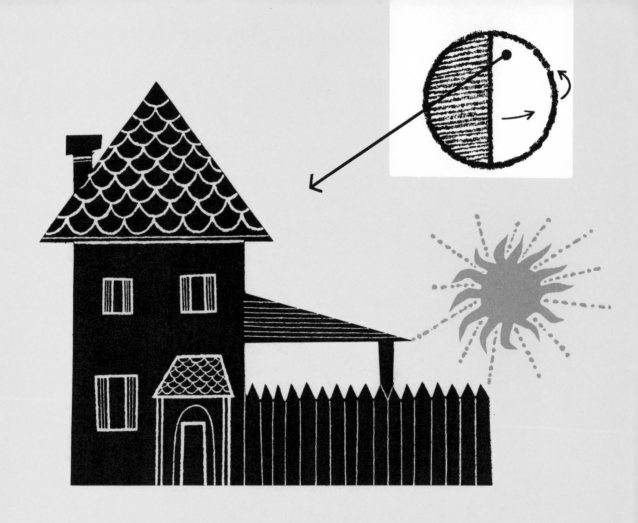

Day comes to your house when your half of the earth
moves into sunlight.

Night comes to your house when your half of the earth moves out of sunlight.

You can find this out for yourself.

Do this experiment.

Play that you are the earth.

Pretend a lamp is the sun.

Stand so your left side is toward the lamp.

Hold your arms out from your sides.

Your left hand points to the lamp.

The lamp is the sun.

Look toward the lamp. This is sunrise.

Turn to your left toward the lamp, but stay on the
same spot.
Keep your arms out from your sides.
Now look at the lamp. This is day.

Keep turning.
Your right hand points to the lamp.
Now look toward the lamp. This is sunset.

Keep turning. Now your back is toward the lamp. This is night.

You turned around once. You had sunrise, day, sunset, and night.

When the earth turns around once, your house has sunrise, day, sunset, and night. And you have sunrise, day, sunset and night.

Watch the sun.
In the morning, the earth carries
   you toward the sunlight.
You have sunrise.

In the afternoon, the earth carries you away from the sunlight. You have sunset.

Now you know:

The earth looks like a big ball.

The earth is a sphere.

The earth turns all the time.

The earth is turning all day while you are awake.

It turns once in a day.

The earth is turning all night while you are asleep.

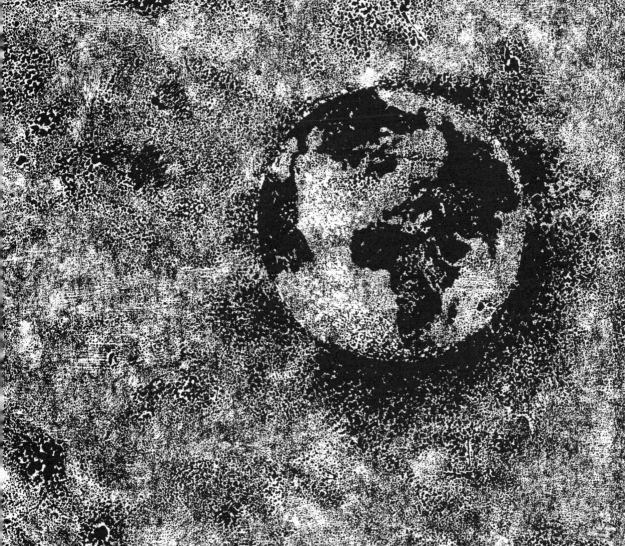

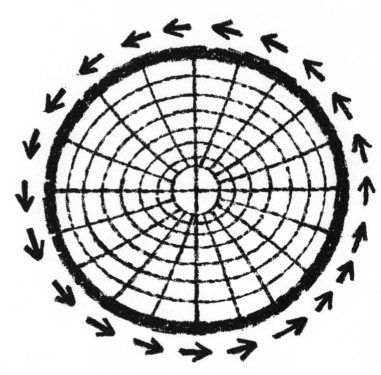

You have day and night because the earth turns.
You have sunrise and sunset because the earth turns.

ABOUT THE AUTHOR

FRANKLYN M. BRANLEY is Chairman and Astronomer at the American Museum-Hayden Planetarium where he has contact with audiences of all ages and where he directs the diverse educational program. For many years he has helped children learn scientific facts and principles at an early age without impairing their sense of wonder about the world they live in. Before coming to the Planetarium, Dr. Branley taught science at many grade levels including the lower elementary grades, high school, college, and graduate school.

Dr. Branley received his training for teaching at the State University College at New Paltz, New York, at New York University, and Columbia University. He lives in Woodcliff Lake, New Jersey.

ABOUT THE ARTIST

HELEN BORTEN has illustrated several books for children and is the author and illustrator of two others: *Do You See What I See?* and *Do You Hear What I Hear?*

Mrs. Borten was born in Philadelphia, Pennsylvania, and was graduated from the Philadelphia Museum College of Art. She lives in Lafayette Hill, Pennsylvania.